Ig Ismaeel

تَسْهِيلُ الأَخْلَاقِ وَالآدَابْ

TAS-HEELUL AKHLAAQ WAL AADAAB

2

Tasheel-ul-Aadaab Wal Akhlaaq Level 2

First Impression 2004
Second Impression 2008

Jamiatul Ulama Taalimi Board:
Curriculum Development Committee

1st Floor, Baitul Hamd,
32 Dolly Rathebe Road,
Fordsburg 2092,
South Africa
E-mail: taalimi@islamsa.org.za

As with any educational material, the contributors have been influenced by a number of people to whom they have spoken and books they have read. The contributors acknowledge this with appreciation.

The Curriculum Development Committee have made every effort to ensure accuracy.

A copy of the British Library Cataloguing-in-Publication Data is available from the British Library.

ISBN: 1-919942-10-6

Design: Stratford Design UK

Contents

Bismillahir Rahmaanir Raheem بسم الله الرحمن الرحيم

INTRODUCTION TO *AKHLAAQ*

Allaah ﷻ has created man in the best of forms and as the best of creation. He sent Nabee Muhammad ﷺ to perfect the character of mankind. In order to live as decent human beings, we need to have good manners regarding our own conduct and regarding other people. This is known as having good *Akhlaaq* / character. A person with good *Akhlaaq* is always clean, respectful, honest, and caring. He is loved by Allaah ﷻ and liked by people. People feel safe from the evil of his tongue and hands. He himself enjoys a peaceful life and he makes it possible for others to do the same. The difference between human beings and animals is that human beings lead their lives based on mercy and respect, while animals lead their lives based on power and strength. When people fail to bring good *Akhlaaq* in their lives, they become worse than animals.

Nabee Muhammad ﷺ had the best of character and was sent by Allaah ﷻ to teach us noble Character.

Nabee Muhammad ﷺ said that:

"I have been sent to perfect good character."

Muslim manners are derived from the teachings of Allaah ﷻ and His Nabee ﷺ. The noble character of Nabee ﷺ is based on the Qur'aan. If we follow his example we will be following the Qur'aan. Nabee ﷺ has said that: *"Fear of Allaah and good manners will admit us into Jannah."*

Muslim manners do not change with time nor go out of fashion. Muslim manners are for everybody; the rich, poor, male, female, young and old. A Muslim's conduct must first touch those nearest to him, his family, and neighbours.

Lesson one When I go to learn

When a student leaves home to learn, he is in the path of Allaah until he returns home. Learning is an act of ‘Ibaadah, which must be carried out with certain rules. Cleanliness, respect, and punctuality are the three golden rules for every student. We must be clean, and our books must be neat. We respect our teachers. We do our work on time.

1. I wash and brush my teeth.
2. I wear clean clothes.
3. I wear clothes that show I am a respectful student and that are according to the rules of my madrasah.
4. I clean my shoes and comb my hair.
5. I have a healthy meal.
6. I make sure that I have the right books for my lessons.
7. I hug my mummy and daddy and leave by making salaam.
8. I make sure that I am not late for madrasah or school.
9. I carry my Qur'aan and books with respect.

Story one Learning

Keen Interest In Learning

Long ago there was a great Islamic scholar. He was known as Imam Malik. Imam Malik gave lessons of the Qur'aan and the Hadeeth of Rasul Sallalahu Alaihi wa Sallam. Students from far and near came to learn from him. One of his students, Yahya, had come all the way from Spain to Madina to acquire Islamic knowledge from him.

One day when Imam Malik was giving lessons, a crowd passed by shouting, 'an Elephant, an Elephant.' Elephants being rare in Arabia, all of Imaam Malik's pupils rushed out of the classroom in their curiosity to see the strange creature.

Yahya however, did not move from his place. Imam Malik asked him why he too was not curious to see the elephant which is not found in Spain. "Respected Muallim," replied Yahya, "I have come here from such a distant land not to see an elephant, but to learn from you and stay in your company to gain knowledge."

Imam Malik was very much pleased with this reply. He smiled and said, "You are a very intelligent boy." Imam Malik said these words with such sincere affection that Allaah, in his mercy, made Yahya a great and intelligent scholar of Spain.

Lesson two Greed

Muslims prefer others above themselves, even if they get less. They find happiness in fulfilling the needs of others. A Muslim is one who loves for his brother what he loves for himself. He is not selfish, nor greedy. Greed makes a person stingy and jealous.

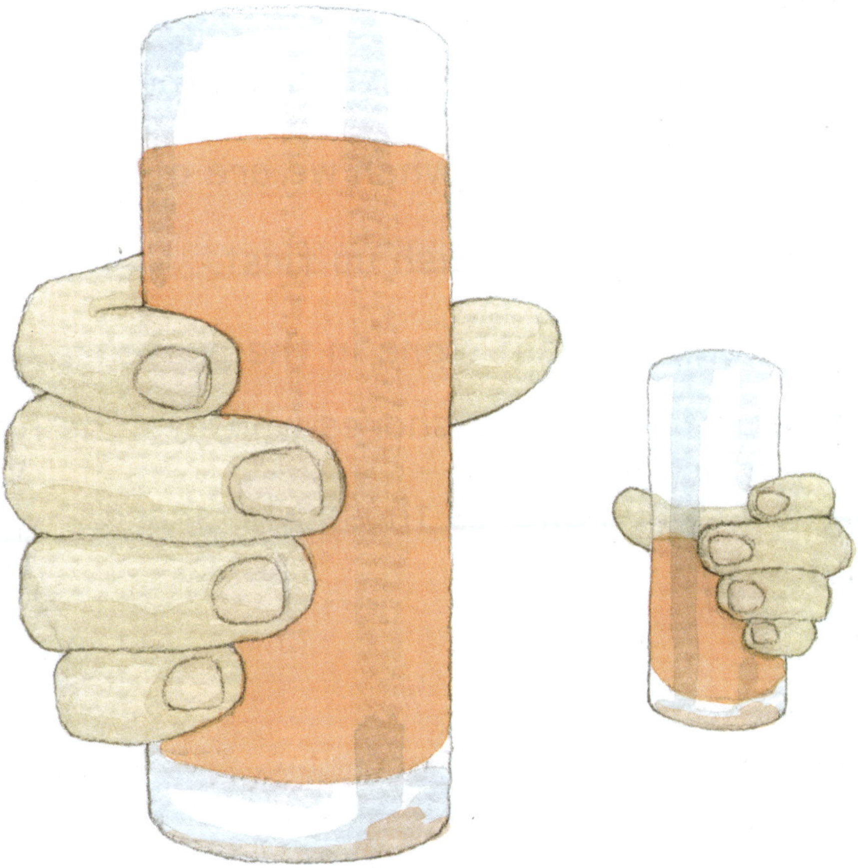

1. A greedy person is never satisfied and always want more.
2. A greedy person does not care for the feelings and needs of other persons.
3. A greedy person is generally disliked.
4. Greed makes a person unmindful of the Hereafter.
5. We must not be greedy when we are offered food.
6. Always allow others to dish up first.
7. A Muslim does not eat alone in the presence of other people. He always shares whatever he has.
8. Allaah loves and rewards those who share.

Story two Greed

Take As Much As You Can Hold

Once upon a time a boy saw a jar lying on the road side. It had a narrow neck and was full of nuts. The boy saw the nuts and felt like taking them. So, he put his hand into the jar and held as many nuts as his hand could grasp. But when he tried to pull it out, he could not do so.

The boy was not ready to lose the nuts at all though he was unable to take his hand along with them. So, he felt disappointed and began to weep.

A man was looking at the boy from a distance. He lost no time to know where the trouble lay. He came near the boy and said, "Don't be so greedy, my son. Be content with half the nuts at one time. You will be able to get your hand out. If you want more, you can have them with a second try."

The boy followed the point and acted upon the man's advice. He was happy to get the nuts. So, he thanked the man and went away.

Lesson three Pets

Nabee ﷺ has taught us to be kind towards the creation of Allaah, even animals. Pets are helpless creatures who depend on our mercy and care. If we keep a pet then we must make sure no harm or difficulty comes to that pet. Allaah ﷻ becomes displeased with us if we cause suffering to our pets. Nabee ﷺ told his companions that Allaah punished a woman who allowed her cat to starve, while he forgave another woman because she gave water to a very thirsty dog. (Bukhaaree and Muslim)

1. We provide a comfortable place for our pets to live.
2. We make sure there is enough food and water for our pets.
3. We nurse them when they become sick.
4. We never kick, hit or throw our pets.
5. We must not frighten our pets.
6. We do not allow our pets to sleep with us.
7. We must always wash our hands after touching or playing with our pets.
8. We do not keep dogs or any wild animals as pets. Dogs can be kept to guard our homes and properties.

Story three Cruelty to Animals

Cruel Fun Is No Fun At All

Once upon a time there was a big pool of water near a village. It abounded with frogs. The village children played near the pool everyday in the evening.

One day some small boys came to play near the pool. Suddenly one of them saw a few frogs swimming about in the shallow water. He felt amused to see them. Calling his play-mates, he said to them, "What fun it will be to pelt stones at these frogs! They will run about to save themselves."

So, the boys started pelting stones at the poor frogs ruthlessly. They were laughing aloud while doing so. As a result, several frogs lost their lives. Seeing them lying dead, the boys laughed even louder.

At last, a young frog popped its head out of the water and said, "Oh, stop! That's enough. I beg you to stop this fun. You don't know, your cruel sport means death to us."

Hearing the frog's words, the boys ran away.

Lesson four Relatives

Allaah has commanded us to be good and kind to our relatives. Our relatives include our uncles, aunts and cousins. Allaah is kind to those who are kind to their relatives. Nabee ﷺ has said, He who breaks off relations (with his relatives) will not enter Jannah. (Bukhaaree and Muslim) Our relatives help us in times of difficulty. Good family relations also strengthens the Ummah of Nabee ﷺ.

1. We must visit our relatives and invite them to visit us.
2. If we are unable to visit them, we must keep in touch with them.
3. We must even keep in touch with relatives who break relations.
4. Allaah gives us double reward if we give charity to our poor relatives.
5. We must visit them when they are sick.
6. We must help them when they are in difficulty and make dua for them.
7. We must also take part in their happy occasions.
8. Gifts to relatives increases love among them.

Story four Relatives

Once Sauleh decided to visit his brother Yahya. Yahya was a very generous person. He treated Sauleh well. His brother asked him how he was. To which he replied: "I am in trouble."

"Why?" asked Yahya.

Sauleh said, "I owe money to a person who is demanding that I pay it back right now. I don't have any money, so how can I repay him? I know you are always generous. That is why I decided to come to you. I hope you can help me, Insha Allaah."

Without any further questions, Yahya got up and gave him the money. Sauleh was overjoyed at Yahya's generosity.

After he left, Yahya cried.

"Why didn't you simply apologize and make some excuse. You did not have to give him anything," said his wife.

"No! I'm not crying because he took my money. Rather I'm crying because I should have known about the difficult condition that he was in and I should have helped him before he asked," Yahya told his wife.

He sat down very quietly and then called out to his wife, "in the future we should try to be more caring about our family and relatives."

Remember to be caring to those near to you first.

Lesson five The Poor and Needy

Islaam has commanded the strong to help the weak, and the rich to help the poor. Nabee ﷺ has said, Allaah will not show mercy to those who do not show mercy to others. (Bukhaaree, Muslim) Allaah helps a person as long as he helps his fellow brother. Helping the poor and needy unites the community and brings about peace.

1. All human beings are the family of Allaah.
2. We must help each other as members of one large family.
3. We help the poor and needy by giving them money.
4. We feed the poor, clothe the naked, and give shelter to the homeless.
5. We speak kind words to them and comfort them in times of difficulty.
6. We visit them and help them with their household duties.
7. We do not remind them of our favours to them.
8. We serve them sincerely, for the pleasure of Allaah and do not tell people about it.
9. We take special care of widows.
10. We help widows by doing their shopping and housework.

Story five The Poor and Needy

Umar رَضِيَ اللّٰهُ عَنْهُ helping widows

Once when Sayadinna Umar رَضِيَ اللّٰهُ عَنْهُ was patrolling the streets of Madinah he spotted a tent on the outskirts. When he went to the tent he saw a woman with children. He noticed the children were crying and there was a pot on the fire. He asked the woman why the children were crying. She replied it was due to hunger. Sayadinna Umar رَضِيَ اللّٰهُ عَنْهُ asked her what was in the pot. She told him it was only water to show the children that food was being prepared.

Sayadinna Umar رَضِيَ اللّٰهُ عَنْهُ hurried to Madinah to the Baitul Maal to fetch flour, dates and other things to prepare a meal. He carried the food on his back as he himself prepared the meal and gave it to the woman to feed the children. The lady was very pleased with Sayadinna Umar's رَضِيَ اللّٰهُ عَنْهُ kindness and she made dua for him.

Lesson six Orphans

Children who do not have parents need our special care. Nabee ﷺ was an orphan and has promised those who care for orphans to be very close to him in Jannah. He said that "the best home among Muslims is a home in which an orphan is treated with kindness." (Ibn Majah)

1. The life of a child who does not have parents is very difficult.
2. He does not have a mother to care for him or a father to provide for him.
3. It is our duty to show love, care and kindness to them.
4. Orphans are very special people who deserve special treatment.
5. We must not fight with them or say any hurtful things to them.
6. We share our belongings with them and make them feel like our very own brothers and sisters.
7. We should make them feel special by sending gifts to them.

Story six Orphans

Sympathy Towards The Orphans

Hatim Tai is renowned for his generosity. And from his family a great and revered saint emerged known as Dawood Tai.

For quite a few days Dawood Tai had not tasted meat. One day he decided to have his desire fulfilled. Accordingly he bought some mutton. The maid servant prepared a delicious meat-curry for him. When the food was served before him, Dawood Tai thought of some orphan children of his locality and asked the maid about their condition.

The maid servant replied:

"They are suffering from the pangs of poverty. Allaah alone knows when their condition will take a turn for the better."

Thereupon Dawood said: "In that case these unfortunate children may not have the opportunity to taste meat, take this dish away from me and feed these poor unfortunate kids."

The maid replied: "you too have not partaken of the meat for a number of days. Why not you enjoy it yourself? These kids will be fed on some other day."

"No, I shall not eat it," replied the great man, "You better feed them only. The meat they eat shall reach Allaah whereas whatever I eat will be rubbed in dust."

So saying, he sent the cooked delicious meat to feed the orphans, even though he had himself longed for it.

Lesson seven Sleep

Sleep is a blessing from Allaah. It is a form of rest and helps us to continue with our work. We must sleep early and wake up early. Too little sleep makes it difficult for us to pay attention and is unhealthy.

1. We make Wudhu and brush our teeth before going to bed.
2. We hug our parents and make Salaam before going to bed.
3. We dust out beds before getting into them.
4. We dress decently when going to sleep.
5. We read the dua before sleeping and when waking up.
6. We think of all the wrong things we did in the day and ask Allaah to forgive us.
7. We sleep on our right side with our right palm under our right cheek.
8. We do not sleep on our stomachs.

Story seven Sleep

Sameer lived on a farm with his parents. The night before he went out to look for the crescent moon of Ramadaan which he saw. He went to bed very excited, read his dua and was soon fast asleep.

"Wake up, wake up Sameer," his mother called out. It is time for Suhoor. He woke up but as soon as his mother was out of the room, he went back to sleep. His mother did this twice and thereafter decided to leave him alone as he did not get up.

That morning he woke up as usual readying himself for school. He went to the kitchen for breakfast, the table was bare and he found no one there.

He went out looking for mummy who was out feeding the farmyard animals.

Sameer asked "mum! Where is my breakfast?" she replied: darling have you forgotten that there will be nothing to eat until sunset, as it is Ramadaan.

Sameer now remembered and felt very guilty. Everything was falling into place. He went to school. Everyone in his class was fasting. He was very upset. At school he learnt about Ramadaan.

He came from school and did not ask his mom for food.

At the time of Asr Salaah, he made wudhu and went to the Masjid. He stayed there until Maghrib.

That night he was very quiet and after Salaah he woke up his mum and whispered.

“Please wake me up for Suhoor, I promise I won’t go back to sleep.”

“Insha Allaah!” Replied his mum.

He went to sleep happily knowing that his mummy would wake him up.

He lay on the right side, read his dua and was soon fast asleep.

Lesson eight Visiting

Allaah rewards us for visiting our families, friends and neighbours. We also visit the sick, our teachers and people who are in difficulty. Visiting each other creates love between people. Nabee ﷺ said that: "when two Muslims meet each other for the sake of Allaah, their sins are forgiven before they leave each other." (Ahmad, Muslim, Ibn Majah)

1. We knock on the door and seek permission to enter.
2. If after knocking for the third time, we do not receive a reply, we leave.
3. We do not visit at odd hours.
4. We make salaam to the person who answers the door.
5. We sit respectfully and do not ask for anything.
6. We do not interrupt when the elders are talking.
7. We say Jazakumullah when we are offered something to eat and we do not act greedily.
8. We welcome visitors to our home with a smile.
9. We respect our visitors and offer them something to eat or drink.
10. We walk with our visitors to the door when they leave.

Story eight Visitors

It was the beginning of the weekend.

Rasheed was very excited. His dad told him that they were going to see his cousins who lived in a nearby town. In his excitement he did everything that he was not supposed to have done.

Can you help little Rasheed telling him what he has done is not correct and what he should have done instead.

On arriving at his uncle Dawood's home he jumped out of the car and ran straight into the house he did not wait for his mom and dad to get off.

He went straight to cousin Aaliyaas' room and helped take out all her games. When she came into the room she was upset at what she saw.

It was not long after when his aunt called them in for meals.

He stopped what he was doing rushed to the table and dished out a large amount of food. He was about to finish it and then saw some chocolate cake, which he gobbled up.

His dad and uncle were talking and he kept on interrupting.

Not longer after he got caught up in a fight with his cousins.

Soon it was time for them to go home. Rasheed had done so many things that he should not have done.

Can you help him so that he does not do it again.

Lesson nine Play

There is a time to work and a time to play. We all like to play and have fun. Play makes us fresh and gives us the strength to carry on with our work. Too much play makes us lazy and causes us to lose interest in our work.

1. We must first do our work before going out to play.
2. We do not swear or fight when playing.
3. We must play with children who are well behaved.
4. We play with children of our age.
5. We must not cheat when playing a game.
6. We must always play in places where we are safe from harm and danger.
7. We do not play games that are dangerous and could cause us injury.
8. Boys must play on their own, and girls must play on their own.
9. We must play with friends who are our age.
10. When the Athaan is called out we must stop our play and read our Salaah.

Story nine Play

It was Friday night and Rookeya and Ebrahim were very happy that there was no school and madrassah the next day.

All they wanted to do was to play. Although their Mum said that they are required to rest, they did not listen. They played till late into the night and did not want to listen to their parents.

Mum and Dad warned that they would be tired and not be able to get up for Fajr salaah, but they continued playing.

The next morning they were not able to get up for Fajr salaah and the whole day they felt tired and miserable.

From then, they decided that they had to go early to bed, early to rise, so that they would please Allaah تَعَالَى and do all their work.

Story Play

Zubair barged into aunty Shireen's house screaming "Where is Bilaal, where is Bilaal". Aunty Shireen who was baking, came to the door and asked him what he wanted. He just pushed her aside and went straight to Bilaal's room, though Bilaal was not there. Uncle Ahmed was busy on the phone and Zubair once again shouted, "Where is Bilaal", and uncle Ahmed shrugged his shoulders, aunty Shireen who in the meantime followed him, asked him to sit down and wait as Bilaal had just gone into the shower. In the meantime she offered Bilaal one of the freshly baked biscuits but instead he took a whole hand full and stuffed them in his mouth. He did not look at her and continued gulping the biscuits down. A few minutes later he got tired of waiting and left the house without telling anyone.

Question

Tell us of all the things that Zubair did that were not right ?

Notes to the Muallim/ah

- This book has nine lessons.

- SUGGESTED DEVELOPMENT OF LESSON TO COVER THE FIRST SECTION OF THE SYLLABUS
  - Story for each lesson
  - The notes in the 'block' serves as an introduction to the lesson. These are not intended for the learners, but rather be used by the Muallim/ah in the development of the lesson.

Period 1:

Introduce the lesson to the learners, using the 'blocked' information as a guide.

Period 2 & 3:

Explain the keypoints to the learners. Remember to engage learners, as they will respond accordingly. The Mualim/ah to expand on each point and make it interesting.

Period 4:

Read the story to the children. They will be able to identify what they see as right and wrong, as this will become a basis for your revision.